ti Kay Nou

Copyright © 2013 by Elma Julia Felix

Photography © 2012 - 2013 by Elma Julia Felix

All rights reserved. No part of this publication may be reproduced, distributed, or transmitted in any form or by any means, including photocopying, recording, or other electronic or mechanical methods, without the prior written permission of the publisher, except in the case of brief quotations embodied in critical reviews and certain other noncommercial uses permitted by copyright law.

Portions of this project have been funded in part by The Bank of Nova Scotia, Saint Lucia Limited and Saint Lucia Electricity Services, Limited.

Excerpt from 'The Antilles: Fragments of Epic Memory' Nobel Lecture, December 7, 1992 © The Nobel Foundation 1992. Reprinted by permission from The Nobel Foundation and the Honourable Derek Walcott.

Cataloging-in-Publication data
Felix, Elma, J.
 Ti Kay Nou : an uplifting journey through our tiny Saint Lucian houses / Elma Julia Felix : Foreword by Milton Eric Branford, Sr.
 p. cm.
 ISBN 978-0-9893427-1-1

First Edition, Paperback, 2013

Author: Elma Julia Felix
Editor: Kelly McNees
Design & Layout: Elma Julia Felix
Watercolour Aerials: © Christopher Podstawski
Photos: © Elma Julia Felix

Dedicated to the people of Saint Lucia; to their past, present and future.

donors

The vision of Ti Kay Nou could not have been achieved without the generous support of those listed below, demonstrating their interest in and appreciation for Saint Lucia and the architectural heritage that surrounds us.

The Bank of Nova Scotia Saint Lucia Limited

Saint Lucia Electricity Services Limited

acknowledgements

Compiling this book has been a rewarding experience which has enriched my journey into the built heritage of Saint Lucia. The true heroes of this book are the owners and caretakers of the Ti Kay; those who have commissioned them, restored them, maintained and preserved the memory of them. To the many residents who let me photograph their homes and were generous enough to share their stories; Her Excellency Dame Pearlette Louisy and the Louisy Family, Jonah George, Ma Bella, Marie Gustave aka Ms. Cook, John Simon aka Jah Lamb, Margherita Alexander, Guy Fevrier, Eldon Marthurin, and those who granted permission for photographs. My interactions with you have been extremely rewarding, and your memories have added a new dimension to this publication, thank you.

I am deeply grateful to the Honourable Derek Walcott and The Nobel Foundation for allowing me to use excerpts of The Antilles: Fragments of Epic Memory for this publication.

Mr. Eric Branford Sr., I thank you for taking the time to share your insurmountable knowledge of Saint Lucian history with me. You have inspired me with your unshakable belief; Ti Kay Nou wouldn't have been possible without your assistance and dedication. I will forever treasure the hours upon hours of conversations we've shared. Many thanks to the staff of the Saint Lucia Archeological and Historical Society, who helped locate files on my behalf.

Finding historical facts and details were essential in achieving the completed publication, and I was fortunate to have the help of several people. Robert Devaux, you are a legend in your own right, and your memory lives with us forever. Thank you for your early guidance and encouragement; the memory of our conversations will stay with me always. John Robert Lee, thank you for always pointing me in the right direction, with a never ending list of resources. For archival information, I am indebted to the Saint Lucia National Trust and The Saint Lucia National Archives. Dawn French, your foresight about the direction of architecture in Saint Lucia is still valid 25 years later. Thank you for granting me permission to use excerpts of your article for this publication.

Shay Cozier, we're artists who love what we do, and although others may not understand our vision at first, it is important that we believe in ourselves, and our work. Thank you for your encouragement you've been an inspiration in more ways than one.

A few very special friends deserve recognition for always providing shoulders to lean on, having patience during periods of intense research and providing amusement during writing hibernation. Jason Gadson, Eishnel

Henry, Larry Monrose, Nadela Noel and Michelle Smith, thank you all for being amazing friends. To Stephen Johnson who provided early insight, ideas and encouragement as the early concept of Ti Kay Nou. I couldn't have done without you. To Robin, thank you for giving me the motivation years ago to start this venture when I thought I couldn't. To Trestian Stewart, who took care of my Miami affairs while I was away photographing, thank you. To my Dover, Kohl and Partners family, thank you for being supportive to me in this effort.

I am indebted to my wonderful editor Kelly McNees for her hard work, invaluable suggestions and advice. Linley Spooner and Hannes Robertze, thank you for your keen eyes and photography insight. Kirk Elliott and John Darley of IDEA Orlando, thank you for assisting with acquiring necessary aerial imagery. To Christopher Podstawski, thank you for re-creating the amazing aerials, Ti Kay Nou wouldn't be the same without them!

To my family, who for countless hours engaged me in conversation, spared the time to accompany me on various visits and photography shoots across the island; I am thankful to you for your help and constant encouragement. I would like to express my deep and sincere thanks to Marcelda Auguste, Esther Boodha, Eugenia Soudin and Charles Cadet.

A very special thank you to Nigel Dudley, for the effort, encouragement and inexorable support you have given me over the life of Ti Kay Nou. Thank you for believing in me more than I believed in myself at times, and for giving me a nudge when it was needed. Thank you for always being there; I am forever grateful to you.

To my parents; there are not enough pages or words in the English language to thank you. You have shown incredible love, guidance and support on this journey. Thank you for everything you have done; hunting owners down, helping to post pictures on my wall, to taking pictures. You have taught me that if I tiptoe high enough, I can reach the stars. I love you both, thank you.

contents

Excerpt from The Antilles:
Fragments of Epic Memory *by* Honourable Derek Walcott ... vi

Foreword *by* Milton Eric Branford Sr. ... ix

Letter to the Reader ... x

Introduction ... 1

Common Building Types ... 6

Quatier de Gros Islet ... 9

Quatier de Babonneau ... 21

Quatier de Castries ... 29

Quatier de Anse La Raye ... 49

Quatier de Canaries ... 61

Quatier de Soufrière ... 73

Quatier de Choiseul ... 89

Quatier de Laborie ... 97

Quatier de Vieux Fort ... 109

Quatier de Micoud ... 119

Quatier de Dennery ... 125

Glossary ... 130

Historic Preservation in Saint Lucia ... 132

the antilles: fragments of epic memory
by Honourable Derek Walcott, OBE OCC

Before it is all gone, before only a few valleys are left, pockets of an older life, before development turns every artist into an anthropologist or folklorist, there are still cherishable places, little valleys that do not echo with ideas, a simplicity of rebeginnings, not yet corrupted by the dangers of change. Not nostalgic sites but occluded sanctities as common and simple as their sunlight. Places as threatened by this prose as a headland is by the bulldozer or a sea almond grove by the surveyor's string, or from blight, the mountain laurel.

One last epiphany: A basic stone church in a thick valley outside Soufrière, the hills almost shoving the houses around into a brown river, a sunlight that looks oily on the leaves, a backward place, unimportant, and one now being corrupted into significance by this prose. The idea is not to hallow or invest the place with anything, not even memory. African children in Sunday frocks come down the ordinary concrete steps into the church, banana leaves hang and glisten, a truck is parked in a yard, and old women totter towards the entrance. Here is where a real fresco should be painted, one without importance, but one with real faith, mapless, Historyless.

How quickly it could all disappear! And how it is beginning to drive us further into where we hope are impenetrable places, green secrets at the end of bad roads, headlands where the next view is not of a hotel but of some long beach without a figure and the hanging question of some fisherman's smoke at its far end. The Caribbean is not an idyll, not to its natives. They draw their working strength from it organically, like trees, like the sea almond or the spice laurel of the heights. Its peasantry and its fishermen are not there to be loved or even photographed; they are trees who sweat, and whose bark is filmed with salt, but every day on some island, rootless trees in suits are signing favorable tax breaks with entrepreneurs, poisoning the sea almond and the spice laurel of the mountains to their roots. A morning could come in which governments might ask what happened not merely to the forests and the bays but to a whole people.

foreword by Milton Eric Branford Sr., SLMM

In this book, Ti Kay Nou, architectural history is examined from the human perspective. In an age where technology is rapidly accelerating, the author, Elma Julia Felix, has brought back to life what most architects overlook. Ti Kay Nou, is a well-defined research of the structure and significance of early dwellings in Saint Lucia. The book sheds a new light on the skills and techniques employed in the construction of these buildings, giving a fresh interpretation of their use which will no doubt enhance the political, cultural and social objectives for future architects.

In this rich, insightful book, Felix examines and evaluate the skills, and technologies of these skillful early builders who understood from their own experience, the possible effects of wind, hurricane, earthquakes, flooding and other natural disasters. Their knowledge of timber and its various qualities, as well as other resource materials used in construction of the desirable building was of paramount importance. All these factors are also researched by Felix.

Ti Kay Nou describes in detail the method of building in the 16th-19th century, where selected timber was cut in the forest and then drawn or hauled to the construction site by a team of neighbours, friends and other helpers. Felix correctly describes this type of building activity as a Coup-de-Main or Koudmen, quite literally, helping hand. The accompanying photographs cover a period of 100-150 years, and show existing buildings that have survived all forms of weather and other hazards. They are illustrations of important historical land marks in the urban and rural areas in the city, towns and villages that deserve the admiration of all.

This fascinating book systematically dissects the early myths of the beautiful façade, improving the understanding of the history of our early shelters. It points the way towards a new interpretation and perspective for today's architects and builders.

All the illustrations are the author's original work drawn from her years of involvement in the study of Saint Lucian culture and architecture. These illustrations are passed on to the reader to further increase their knowledge and understanding of this fascinating subject.

—Milton Eric Branford
Archaeological Secretary and Administrator of the Saint Lucia Archaeological and Historical Society

letter to the reader

In every family throughout time, parents and older relatives have shared stories of the past. They may have shared these tales to amuse themselves and others, comparing their experiences to modern life, or to keep alive a history that might otherwise be lost. Today, the pace of life has changed. We are caught up in the social media age, faces illuminated by bright screens and focused exclusively on the present. There is no time to sit around and listen to these stories now, and we have no time to wonder about our past.

I recall countless stories of a particular place in my family's history, a place where banter, song and good food created the foundation; a tiny vernacular house in Quarte Chemin, Soufrière. My father lived in this house with his grandparents and other siblings when he was a child. I never knew who built the house or its origins—it just felt like home. The house was neatly tucked away and surrounded by thick vegetation. Its kitchen—three stones outside—was where I learned the value of one pot. I still think about those meals today. I've visited the house dozens of times, fascinated by its creaky floor boards to the sound of wind howling through jalousie windows. More memorable are my father's stories of his adventures and hideout spots. To this day, I credit that tiny house for launching my interest in traditional architecture, and quite possibly this book.

On my many trips to Saint Lucia armed with a camera, I ventured out to take pictures of our traditional houses just like my tiny family house, a past-time we can all admit to. Something about them commands our attention.

Every year however, I seemed to find fewer and fewer of them, and I wondered—was anybody else noticing that they were disappearing? It dawned on me that a time would come when someone, somewhere, would want to know about these houses. Fearful that our obsession with the present and more modern way of life might allow the stories of these homes to slip away; *Ti Kay Nou* was born.

Over the years, I've taken more than a thousand images—both film and digital—in an effort to capture what was left. The collection of images in this book show the character and diversity of our small wooden vernacular houses, something we've taken for granted and too easily forgotten.

The houses in this book aren't simply pretty pictures. Each house tells a story of endurance, character, and grace; they are much more than little bits of folklore. The Ti Kay is critical to our identity as people. Today, sadly, most of the dwellings are at risk. Without these remnants of our past, the identity of Saint Lucia will be diminished and our cultural heritage depleted. The Ti Kay was not built by architects or designers—they were built out of the need for practical shelter, making them even more dynamic.

Ti Kay Nou consists of over 70 images which have been carefully placed in the geographic order of Quatiers or Quarters—clockwise from the north, around to the west, south, and east. The images contained in this book

are meant to arouse local awareness and initiate conversations about the role the Ti Kay plays within our society—past and present. Some photographs are accompanied by text, transcribed from dozens of recorded conversations with residents and neighbours. Because this publication cannot include every important Ti Kay in each community, I decided to focus on depicting the best representative images of the island's wonderful tapestry of houses. Since the publication of Ti Kay Nou, conditions have changed for many dwellings—some have fallen deeper into decay, or have been totally demolished.

Each dwelling shown in this publication is for educational purposes only. As an author, I am in no way intending to sell, destroy, tamper with or exploit the houses shown. As there is no legislation preventing someone from taking, I do respect the privacy of owners, and have done my utmost best to seek permission from property owners. It is often difficult to do so, as most of the owners reside overseas, or renters aren't willing to divulge too much information.

I urge readers who plan to visit these houses to remember that the properties presented are private dwellings. Where private properties are visible from a public road, I call attention to them as parts of the traditional architectural landscape; however, I do not by any means invite you to trespass! Please respect the privacy of residents and owners. If you wish to admire, do so from a comfortable distance.

On the last day I spent photographing houses in Castries, I encountered half a dozen young men, red-eyed from a spliff they passed among them, sitting in the verandah of a house on Grass Street. I'm sure they were more than suspicious of a woman armed with a camera, obviously not a neighbor. I introduced myself by saying that I was an architect, taking pictures for a book about traditional houses in Saint Lucia. They laughed in reply. "Dem old houses? Around here full of dem tings—but what you want to know about dem for? Nobody really cares about dat you know, miss." I tried to answer that recurring and most incorrect thought by explaining that we should care about them; they are a vivid part of our culture and history. The story of these dwellings is, indeed, the story of the people who have built Saint Lucia. I finished our conversation by saying that I was writing the book for them. As you can imagine, I got even more laughs, but it turns out they were intrigued. This playful banter led to a few pictures with new friends, and permission for an image shown in this book. He has fond memories of this house; his grandmother raised him here and his memories are endless. That day reminded my why Ti Kay Nou is important: It reminds us of our true-built heritage—and even if for a moment—initiates a conversation about how we used to live.

In the event that you come across a house which isn't included here, or you know the history of a Ti Kay found within the pages of this book—please share it with me on the website; www.tikaynou.com, as this is an ongoing body of work. Who knows, there might be a Ti Kay Nou Two in the beginnings! It is my hope that this publication will initiate conversation between you, members of your family, colleagues and those within the St. Lucian diaspora, to remind us all about these hidden gems which hold so much history and character. It has opened my eyes to a whole new architectural language, I hope it will do the same for you. Enjoy the journey.

an introduction to where people live | kay moun ka wèsté

Saint Lucia, whether approached from the air or sea, is as mysterious and beautiful as its nickname implies: the "Helen of the West." From its first inhabitants, Saint Lucia has charmed many. It is no wonder why this fair isle was at the centre of the most bitter discord between the British and the French for over 150 years. Much has been written about this island's history; it's bloody battles, the devastating natural disasters that, without warning, wiped out everything in their paths, the mysteries behind Saint Lucia's place names, ancient hieroglyphs and stoneware, but where and how did we live?

History tells us that the Amerindians inhabited this island before our colonial settlers. Their architecture was basic, and described at length by early travelers. Basic shelter was all that the Arawaks and Caribs needed. There was no point in building permanent houses because they moved to new and more fertile gardening plots every few years. Their houses were round with steep thatched roofs made of palm leaves and branches. Larger houses in the village had a covered porch before the door. The largest house in the village belonged to the Cacique or Ouboutu. This house was rectangular and held several rooms. Besides these early indigenous structures, the architecture of Saint Lucia, especially its domestic architecture and grand urban places, was largely ignored. A. W. Ackworth writes:

"At Castries, the Anglican Church, dating back from 1834, is a classical composition of some architectural merit, and the Prison (formerly a Barracks) is a well-constructed building of somewhat earlier date (1824-27). But that is about all."

In most of the Windward Islands this sort of chronicle is fairly common. Early travelers recorded their observations primarily about fortifications and military interventions; very rarely did they reflect or comment on the actual architecture they observed. The fragmented bits of literature and research on the subject, and more specifically on historically significant buildings, completely lack detailed descriptions. A narrative written by Henry H. Breen in 1844 describes:

"The streets are wide and well laid out, extending in parallel lines from east to west and from north to south. Most of them are paved, and some are ornamented with foot-paths. The upper part, or Chausée division, is chiefly occupied by the humbler orders, and the houses are all built of wood and covered with shingles. The lower, or Bord-de-mer division, is the resort of the wealthier classes. Here the houses are constructed of stone, brick or wood, according to the taste of the owners, or the prevailing anxiety to guard against the consequences of fire, hurricane or earthquake."

Elsewhere in the Caribbean, settlers made brief notes about what they were seeing on other islands and the commonalities that exist between them. Edward Doran's brief review of the West Indian Hip-Roofed Cottage describes a basic rectangular cottage common to all islands;

"Evidence suggests that the house probably originated within a hundred miles of the English Channel, that it was first introduced into the islands between 1625 and 1700, and that it has been re-diffused among the islands in complex patterns since. The house is always rectangular in plan, and frequently is twice as long as it is wide."

What else do we know about these houses? How were they built and by whom? Latter fragments of literature and excerpts from first-hand accounts paint a picture of the origins of style elements, and give us clues as to how the Ti Kay originated.

origins of architecture

Even if few of the houses in this publication date back more than 100 years, one can still see reflected in the pitch of a roof or the fretwork detailing, some characteristic of imported architecture. The alternation of ownership of Saint Lucia produced a curious mixture of French and Colonial architecture. Vernacular is a term commonly used for dwellings like these. It indicates a combination of the shared characteristics of southern English, French, and West African folk dwellings of the 17th century. We see the influences of these styles, along with tokens of identify that make them uniquely of this island. The importation of architectural styles lagged from pattern books and memory; architectural movements occurring in Europe might not be reflected in local examples until 30 years later, or more. Builder's handbooks offered some help, but frequently they required a translation from traditional European building methods and materials to those available locally. The builders of these houses did not always have a grasp of correct architectural styles and because of this; they rendered some details in unusual ways. The raising of houses off the ground may provide a typical example of the translation of standard foreign concepts into the local vernacular. Builders did this for protection from insects, and, incidentally, to communicate visually the home's importance. The façade of the houses embodies another example. Most contain a door at the centre of the main facade, flanked by windows on either side. This design borrows from the principles of erudite European architecture and is popular in rural architecture in Europe. Raising the house off the ground, fitting it with wooden shingles and large shuttered windows – with its orientation with respect to the prevailing winds – all represent forms of reinterpretation which resulted in the Saint Lucian Ti Kay.

architectural elements

While local builders had to adapt building styles from Europe, they also faced a tedious task of addressing extraordinarily difficult terrain, and do so using abundant materials of wood and stone. Some notable architectural elements developed as a result: local timber boarding or shingle cladding, shutters for protection and privacy, steeply pitched gable roofs for wind resistance, and verandahs that shelter occupants and the building face from sun and rain. These elements didn't only stem from aesthetics. They were developed for purpose and function rather than the "look" alone. A few of these are architectural elements are investigated in the following paragraphs.

the verandah is the most common feature in Caribbean culture, and perhaps one of the only surviving architectural elements in Saint Lucia. Verandah is said to derive from the Hindi word *vara*, to surround with poles. The term may have entered English through the Portuguese, either in India or in Brazil in the seventeenth century. The form was adopted in the late seventeenth century and early eighteenth centuries in the West Indies. That form has remained relatively constant until today. It is characterized by slender pillars, and balustrades decorated with renaissance-inspired fretwork in a wide variety of styles. The verandah adds to the richness of the dwelling's volume and protects the façade from bad weather. Verandahs are always animated by people and brightened with decoration: plants and trinkets. A transitional space between the houses' interior and exterior; the verandah adds privacy, even while permitting residents to share their activities with those passing by. Sheltered in the shade, a person can greet and converse with a neighbor without introducing him or her to the intimacy of the dwelling.

doors and windows

Located around the perimeter of a dwelling, doors and windows combine to create a system of openings allowing light, air and entry into the house. Operable shutters can be attached over door and window openings. They can be closed for privacy and to prevent direct sunlight from entering the building, or left partially open to allow for cross ventilation and light. In addition to being an aesthetically pleasing feature of the home, shutters also protect houses from the damaging gusts of tropical storms and hurricanes. Shutters commonly found in Saint Lucia include jalousie windows—derived from European shutters—these were in use long before their introduction to the West Indies. The word comes from the French word for jealousy, thought to originate from the fact that a resident could adjust the slats in order to look out, but not be seen from the inside. It can be used over window openings, in gables and doorways. Also commonly found in Saint Lucia are solid wooden shutters, which can be quickly and completely closed to protect windows from high winds, heavy rain, and flying debris. Solid shutters can also increase security when closed. A lock installed on the inside of solid shutter panels can decrease the possibility of theft.

fretwork

Fancy interlaced designs, cut out from wood panels and inspired by Victorian examples, decorate the facades and verandahs of houses, sometimes even the interiors. Most of it, if not all of the components of detailed fretwork were handcrafted; machines were rarely used in their creation. Their purpose is to ventilate and protect from the sun, even while providing intricate decoration. No two houses are the same, as each design is a personal expression of the owner. On rare occasions, interior fretwork can be found above partitions between rooms to permit ventilation through the inside of the house.

colour

It is almost impossible to think of the Caribbean without evoking thoughts of brilliant colours: intense red hues of flowers, deep blue skies and sea, a sunset's thousand shades of orange. Before paint was available, the colour of a house was determined by natural materials; wood and stone. Paint was introduced to Saint Lucia between the two world wars, and the vivid colours of the island were soon replicated onto its houses. Colours are typically arranged by twos or threes, creating striking visual contrasts on smaller, more detailed elements. Whether chalky grey from exposed wood, or brightly coloured paint; colour is an essential part of the domestic landscape in Saint Lucia.

entrances & openings

Typically in villages in Saint Lucia, the lot is deeper than it is wide, mostly to accommodate functions at the rear of the house: Washing, gardening, and cooking. Because of this most façades or main entrances to the building are located on the gable end; the triangular portion of a wall between the edges of a sloping roof. When the main entry to the home faces a main road its eaves are decorated with fretwork, and its front door is flanked with windows on either side. As described earlier, the centred façade is inherited from rural architecture in Europe.

the steeple

These mysterious "spiked finials" appear on vernacular houses around the island, and the region. Upon first glance, they appear as decorative ornaments, fixed at the peak of the gable end, over the main entrance. Researchers have disputed its origins for years, and nobody knows its correct origin or meaning; until now. After much research and upon closer inspection at a correctly placed Steeple, or spiked finial, there is always a cross brace at its lower end; turning it into an inverted cross. It is of French and African origin, and as superstition would have it, this inverted cross placed at the main entrance of a dwelling, would protect the contents of the home from evil, and the popular jen gajé (people who practice witchcraft). Elements of non-Christian beliefs and practices persisted after emancipation, and malicious practices seem to have been more radical than normal. It is said that thieves, malicious and evil beings acknowledged the Steeple, and wouldn't dare disrespect it by breaking and entering or harming the habitants inside.

building materials

Wood and stone were both used for constructing the Ti Kay of Saint Lucia, depending on the circumstances and location. Wood predominated, however, and became the very symbol of Saint Lucian architecture. Mixed construction is also common in urban areas within Saint Lucia, and the technique can be understood as a response to the various catastrophes to which the house was exposed to over time. The flexibility of a wooden frame helps it survive earthquakes, but wood is vulnerable to fire. People therefore chose to protect the more vulnerable ground floor from fire by building in stone or masonry, while the upper floor is built of wood. In some cases, wooden shingles were used to cover the exterior of the building. These were made out of *pòwyé* or white cedar. It protected the timber from decay, which increased the lifespan of the exterior.

the Koudmen

In the French West Indies, the Koudmen is the contribution of relatives and neighbours to the construction of a dwelling. It originated from the French expression *Coup de Main* or "helping hand." Born out of hard times, it is a Kwéyol tradition of neighbours helping neighbours through difficult times; natural disasters, fire or sickness. The first recorded Koudmen was by J.T. Rae in 1898;

> "These 'packing-cases' as they were jeeringly termed, are of the most flimsy construction and it would not be difficult to knock a whole house down, especially as the structures rest on four or more big stones. It is no uncommon spectacle to witness one of these Negro huts being carried through the streets by less than a dozen men for the purpose of being deposited on a fresh site"

From the days of carrying a Kay down the street, the Koudmen had turned into a loud and festive gathering - with food, music, dance and storytelling. It did not only aid in house construction, but the Koudmen received a family into the community. From the first till of the soil, to laying corrugated metal sheeting on the roof, residents can rely on the spirit of collaboration that existed within the community. It is a simple humanist philosophy of people caring for each other, knowing that they all belong to something greater; the village.

future of Ti Kay

It is undeniable that in the past few decades, the introduction of concrete has represented a revolution in Saint Lucian architecture. With its advancement though, we see the replacement of traditional architectural elements—and the development of unadapted modernized trends. Concrete symbolizes the powerful image of richness and modernity to residents and is visible on every hilltop, village and town, as concrete pillars rise to the skies.

As the threads to the past wear thinner and thinner with time, Saint Lucia is losing valuable historic architecture at an alarming rate. Our island is not alone, however. Across the Caribbean, a lack of appreciation as well as a scarcity of incentives for historic preservation has resulted in an irreversible loss of historic architecture. Too often, builders consider only demolition when in fact historic elements may be spared with careful planning. An article written by Dawn French in 1988 entitled "A History of Architecture in Saint Lucia and a Projection for the Future," cautions against the unchecked progress of development;

> "Where architecture is concerned, a pause and reflection is needed, and is needed now (1988) or we will soon lose our charm and become another 'Manhattan skyline.' Castries is becoming (or already is) a concrete jungle. Announced proudly by the government as being the most modern in the Caribbean, Castries is a series of boxes, with no character, no reference to who or what we are, where we hope to be. No one wants St. Lucia to be totally swamped by its past, having every building decked in the cosmetics of former ages, but the mass concrete box as it stands does not work on the island. The style must adapt, it must be able to use traditional shapes and materials."

Those conditions still apply to present day, some twenty five years later. Since the process of modernization is irreversible, will the Ti Kay be completely lost? Or will our modern architecture evolve, integrating modern skill with traditional form and function? A conversation about the importance of historic preservation is warranted in Saint Lucia; our historic architecture plays a special role in creating the distinctive character of each and every community. I am not suggesting that we revert to the past; however, we should respect the essential legacy of cultural, educational, recreational, aesthetic, social, and environmental benefits of historic preservation. Our heritage must be preserved for present and future generations.

common building types | konmen kalité kay

type 1

type 2

One of the more commonly found in Saint Lucia, this building type is twice as deep as it is wide. The structures usually have a steep gabled roof with the gabled end at the front facade. Typically, the front entrance occurs on the gable end, usually opening out into the street. A louvered vent sits directly above the door for light and air circulation. Older versions have one-room interiors usually with a partition separating the bedroom from the living room. Washing and cooking activities occurred in the rear-yard of the house.

This building type is a variation of type 1, in that everything has remained the same, except the new addition, or 'wing' to the side of the house. Traditionally, the kitchen was placed at the rear-yard of the house. With the introduction of kerosene stoves in the 1920's the detached kitchen became obsolete. This now meant that the kitchen could be attached directly to the rear or side of the house. The newly attached kitchen still had to be located on the down-wind side of the house to prevent smoke, heat and odors from filling the room. This type also lends itself to making new additions (more rooms) easier, as it's easy to add a room for an expanding family to the rear of the house where the kitchen once stood.

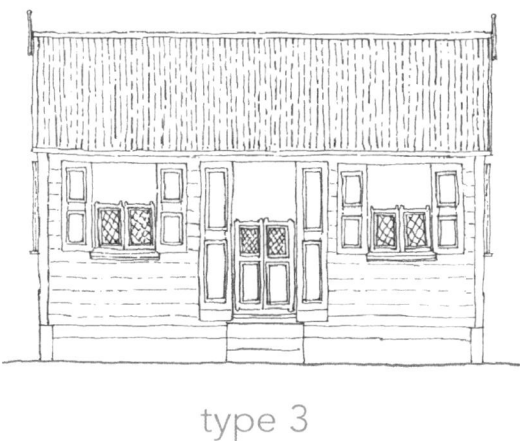

type 3

The front of this building type is always the long side of the building, so the roof ridge runs parallel to the street. The door is located in the centre of the wall space, and is flanked by windows on either side, symmetrically. Asymmetric layouts do exist, but are extremely rare. Because the floor plan is now twice as wide as it is deep, the interior rooms are arranged differently. The front door opens to two rooms, one accommodating the sleeping area, and the other room accommodating all other living activity. Opposite to the front door, another door opens to the rear of the house where cooking and washing occurs.

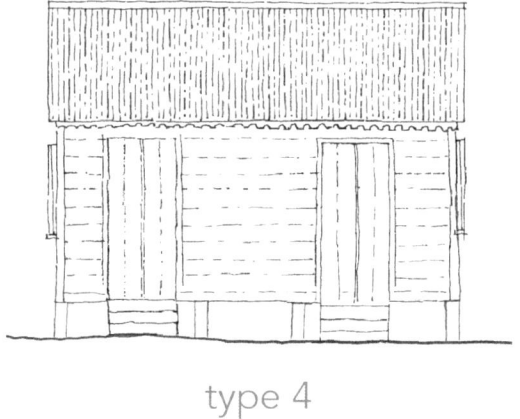

type 4

Type 4 is similar to type 3; it is twice as wide as it is deep. This is the first typology which introduces the concept of a duplex to the island. Some texts refer to this building type as the **Alleyway** or **Passageway** house, and they represent a separate and distinct house type imported onto the island, probably in the latter part of the 19th century. There are two doors, separated on the interior by a partition clearly demarcating two separate living quarters. Each space is private, and usually not larger than one room. Residents can then partition interior spaces with wood or curtains to create personalized spaces or layouts.

the gros islet quarter | quatier de gwosilé

The word islet occurs in old maps and old records of Saint Lucia time and time again. Le Gros Islet is of course the most important—the big islet encompasses the quarter and the village on the shore opposite. As early as 1722, the British were calling Saint Lucia's Gros Islet by the name of Pigeon Island. The Gros Islet bay could easily hold the biggest of ships while cannons on the mainland at Morne Piment could effectively protect the entire bay.

Gros Islet is the administrative centre of the Gros Islet Quarter, a region of Saint Lucia that includes the island's northernmost point, and is the fastest growing quarter on the island. Originally settled by the Caribs, a French map from 1717 provides the first identification of the area as Gros Islet. The community has had a long history of being a Roman Catholic parish, as the first priests who arrived on the island settled in the village in 1749. In modern times, the quarter has continued to flourish. Between 1991 and 2001 the population rose 54% the highest rise in the country. In 2001, the population was 19,409, making it the second most-populous community in Saint Lucia. Many businesses located in the Capital of Castries have moved their services to the North to cater to this growing population.

Notorious for its Friday Night Street Party, Gros Islet's major tourist attraction encompasses several blocks, which are informally cordoned off with the stalls of street vendors. Music, food and dance take over the town for a few hours! When the stalls are packed up and the streets are quiet again, Gros Islet town turns into quite the opposite of its Friday Night Street Party—a slow and sleepy fishing town.

The town is laid on a perfect grid of streets. Its houses are a combination of modern concrete, traditional wooden vernacular, and variations of mixed urban construction. A few small shops dot the town, selling everything from alcoholic beverages to everyday necessities. The Saint Joseph the Worker Roman Catholic Church dominates the town, its structure the tallest and most visible. In 1927, it was decided that the building be constructed in reinforced concrete to defy weather conditions on the very site where the present Church is located. A severe earthquake in 1906 completely destroyed the church which stood in its place.

Pigeon Island, a 44-acre islet connected by a causeway in the 1970s to St. Lucia's west coast, is a beautiful nature park near the town of Gros Islet. It reflects a thousand years of history. There are marked trails with a number of historical sites, like the remains of an 18th-century British fort and Fort Rodney, where the Admiral for which it is named spied on the French ships from its strategic viewpoint.

Rodney Bay named after Fort Rodney, lies south of the main town of Gros Islet, and differs greatly. The areas surrounding the Rodney Bay Village contain shops, a marina, malls, restaurants and night clubs and cater mostly to tourists and young locals.

12 chapel street
OWNER: MA BELLA | CONSTRUCTED IN: 1938

Ma Bella's house is the first photograph I took for Ti Kay Nou, and naturally, she had to be first. Ma Bella is 90-years young—as she says—and has lived in this house her whole life. As we sat down, she hands us confectioneries; gooseberry jam and tamarind balls before we even get started.

"You see behind this house here," she says pointing to the back of the Gros Islet harbor, "all here was swamp." Ma Bella was referring to the Reduit Swamp, which existed when her house was newly built. The swamp has since been filled with earth; hundreds of houses, a state-of-the-art marina, shopping malls and hotels now occupy the reclaimed lands. The entire house was built by hand; even the doors were made by hand – all slats and louvers – not a machine used. The family's yard was located in the rear, along with its kitchen activities.

Ma Bella's house has withstood every hurricane. She jokes that her neighbours shelter within her home during strong storms - a testament at how sturdy this structure is, even in its 90-year-old state. The house was built with **powyé**, or White Cedar, a common wood used in this era. The **powyé** has resisted termites—so far...

The house is one of the most common building types in Saint Lucia. The dwelling is twice as long as it is wide, and the front door occurs within the gable end. The front door opens up to a living room area where Ma Bella welcomes guests. Beyond that, a bedroom and recently constructed concrete kitchen to the rear.

A striking feature of Ma Bella's house is the hand-crafted double door; commonly found within the pages of this book. The double doors allow for the home to be opened to air completely, while still maintaining privacy by protecting those inside from glances from passers-by. All interior doors and partitions are crowned with wooden slats that help keep the house fully ventilated. Because windows are located at opposite ends of one another to allow for cross ventilation, keeping Ma Bella's dwelling completely cool.

Towering next to her house is a newly constructed guesthouse, which has encroached on her privacy. "I can barely keep my windows open, they see all inside my house! There is no reason they should build so tall here." She visited the Ministry of Planning several times to complain, but nothing was done. "I'm sure they want to bulldoze my little house down, **janmen**." Never, she says.

14 | ti kay nou: an uplifting journey through our tiny Saint Lucian houses

ti kay nou: an uplifting journey through our tiny Saint Lucian houses | 17

Wooden shingles protect the houses exterior frame from tropical elements; water, sun and wind. Shingles like these were made of a common wood called ***powyé***, or white cedar. Known for its strength and insect resistance, powye was used for construction of houses as well. Many sculptors use white cedar, they claim it is friendly to their tools and cures well. As demonstrated on the houses shown, shingles are laid from top to bottom, one row tucked under another. Attaching the shingles to the structure required the use of tiny nails.

the babonneau quarter | quatier de babonneau

The hilly district east of Castries, known today as Babonneau, is marked on an 1888 Admiralty map. In Lefort de Latour's description, a certain Babonneau Bonneterre is listed as proprietor of 162 carrès in the vacant Castries quarter. Henry H. Breen mentions J. Babonneau as a vacant succession in 1836.

On the map, Babonneau is roughly three miles from Castries. Some have disputed the origin of its name; most believe that it comes from the French words, **barre-bonne-eau**. In English this would mean 'the ridge of good water'. This may render some truth, because many rivers begin in this area, and Babonneau is home to the island's largest and most important water catchment areas; La Souciere. From the pumping station at Talvern, water is piped to Hill 20 just south of Cabiche. Most of the water for Castries and Babonneau is collected and treated here to make it safe to use.

Babonneau was settled by Joseph Tascher de la Pagerie, who owned an estate in Paix Bouche. He fathered Marie-Joseph Tascher de la Pagerie, better known as Empress Josephine of France, and wife of Napoleon Bonaparte. Because of this deep historical infamy, Babonneau has created new attractions to allow visitors and locals to explore Saint Lucian heritage. The Fond Latisab Creole Park is located within Babonneau, where demonstrations of traditional Saint Lucian way-of-life are on display for the inquisitive visitor and unfamiliar locals. Saint Lucia's oldest sugar plantation, Marquis Plantation, still operates as a working banana estate in the area. Visitors are often drawn to the area to visit Grande Anse beach, where leather back turtles are known to come ashore during breeding season to lay their eggs.

Since the layout of Babonneau is more organic than other quarters on the island, there is no established village centre or rectilinear grid of streets to follow, rather, a single road leads through the village. A quirky intersection—which could be argued as the village's centre—hosts the brightly coloured Good Shepherd Catholic Church, which dates back to 1947. Houses are tucked away from the main road, and surrounded by thick vegetation.

babonneau main road

HOUSE NAME: ROUGH AND SOLID | OWNER: ESTEPHANIE
CONSTRUCTED: 1935

"*Pliché, ich mwen… pliché pou manjé,*" Peel it my child, peel it for you to eat, she said, as she handed my mother a ripe golden apple and a knife. Her name was Estephanie, and we'd spent the afternoon tracking her down in Babonneau. Her house was one I had almost missed, as it was tucked behind bushes and thick foliage, set back at least sixty feet from the main road. She had nothing to offer but a ripe golden apple, as her sign of hospitality.

The house was built by her father in 1923—nothing has been altered since it's construction. She remembers carrying farine to sell; in those days, goods were carried on the head with a *tòch* over long distances. In Estephanie's case, she walked from Babonneau to the Castries Market to sell her farine. She scooped two heaped cups of farine per plastic bag, and they were each sold for six cents.

"*Mwe vann fawine, pou achté galvanniz sa la,*" she said pointing to the original metal sheeting, "*twenty cents pou yonn, I pah janmen lawouj!*" The galvanize she purchased for twenty cents a sheet, never rusted she said. "I just bought new galvanize, and it's more rusty than the old!" pointing at the new pieces, next to the old. No hurricane has ever damaged this house, "when the builder was putting the roof, every time he hit the hammer, he said loud 'Rough and Solid! Rough and Solid!' and from then, I started calling the house that. And look how it's still there. When I die, it will still be there."

Estephanie has no children; and hopes that someone in her family will take interest in the house and save what's left of it.

ti kay nou: an uplifting journey through our tiny Saint Lucian houses

the castries quarter | quatier de kastwi

The name Castries was given to Le Carenage in 1785. The inhabitants of Saint Lucia had asked for the new name to honour a French minister, Charles Eugene Gabriel de la Croix, Marquis de Castries, Marechal de France. The marquisate of Castries, which he inherited when his elder brother died, was situated in the French department (county) of Herault.

Once of the most bustling cities in the Caribbean, Castries, the Capital of Saint Lucia, is alive during the day and turns into a ghost town at night. Castries was founded by the French in 1650 as **Carenage** (meaning safe anchorage), then renamed in 1756 after la Croix commanded a French expeditionary force to Corsica that year. The town grew along the Castries River and the Chaussée Road; described in historic texts as a dirt road raised above the level of the mangroves.

The Capital has been disfigured by four disastrous fires which swept through and erased many examples of early architecture. A few notable pockets of traditional vernacular houses remain in the city, although much of the grid-patterned city centre has been overrun by modern concrete and glass. The famous Rain Restaurant was one of the few architecturally sound larger structures which had survived.

Built during the 19th century, the Catholic Cathedral of the Immaculate Conception is one of the most significant religious buildings built by the French in the Caribbean. Somewhat sober on the outside, it is full of colourful West Indian iconography and murals inside.

One of the major tourist areas in St. Lucia, Castries is a port of call for cruise ships. Cruise ships dock at Pointe Seraphine and La Carenage, two popular duty free shopping centres. The harbor is also served by high-speed catamarans to Guadeloupe, Martinique and Dominica.

Just steps from the cruise ship terminal, the Castries Market offers a local shopping experience. The Castries Market was recently ranked number three in the National Geographic World's Top Ten Food Markets in 2013. Designed and constructed by Bruce & Still Ltd., of Liverpool, and opened in 1894 the market still bustles six days a week under the original red-roofed building. This market is open six days a week and hosts over 200 full-time vendors. It hosts over 200 full-time vendors selling trinkets, souvenirs and fresh produce.

Named after one of St. Lucia's famous Nobel Prize winning poet and playwright, Derek Walcott Square is surrounded by a mixture of traditional vernacular architecture and modern concrete construction. Bordered by Brazil, Micoud, Bourbon and Laborie streets, the oldest parts of Castries can be seen here. Within the square side sits a massive 400-year-old tree that offers shade from the sweltering sun. Though it is a peaceful place today, the square has a turbulent history. In the late 18th century following the French Revolution, it was known as the Place d'Armes, and a guillotine was set up here by Republicans to do away with those who didn't follow the law of the land.

Over the years, the landscape of Castries has transformed into a more modern concrete city. Many buildings tower over fifteen stories high. Haphazard construction occurs regularly, with new buildings encroaching into the public right-of-way; on sidewalks and roads.

7 waterworks road

THE NOOK | OWNER: GUY FEVRIER | CONSTRUCTED: 1924

Affectionately called the Nook by its previous owners, this charming vernacular house sits along Waterworks road on the way to Entrepot, and can easily be missed. Tucked away from the busy main road, the house sits proudly on its lot. Occupying the house is Mr. Guy Fevrier and his Mother, who is 104 years old. They moved into the Nook in 1977.

I did a bit of searching to find the original owners, the Mathurin Family. The Nook was given its name by his father, who built the house in 1923, because of the way it was hidden out of view. There were an abundance of fruit trees in the yard, a small kitchen garden filled with herbs and peppers, ground provisions, "everything except meat and cheese," he said jokingly. In those days, everyone could live off the land, and didn't rely on supermarkets too much. Rice, sugar and flour were bought from small shops located within neighborhoods.

A large cocoa estate—notably the largest cocoa estate in St.. Lucia at the time—was near the current Entrepot Secondary School. "It went on for miles and miles, it was sold to the Government of Saint Lucia for one dollar!" Once the estate was cleared, it changed the atmosphere of the neighborhood dramatically; a housing development and a school were built in its place.

The Nook was built on site, with local builders under the assistance of his father. The family did no renovations to the house, but added on a kitchen in the early 50's. In the nineteenth century, cooking and baking were done in a detached fireside, or kitchen, remote from the house. This practice protected the house from smoke, heat and the danger of accidental fires. The introduction of kerosene stoves in the 1920's rendered the detached kitchen obsolete. This now meant that the kitchen could be attached directly to the rear or side of the house.

On the night of June 21, 1948, the city of Castries burnt to the ground; a catastrophe that has been termed "the greatest calamity to be fall a Colony of its size and resources in so short a space of time," four-fifths of Castries was completely destroyed by fire. Estimated loss was approximately two million pounds.

With everything burnt in the capital, business scrambled to find space to resume operations. The **Saint Lucia Voice** newspaper's building was burnt to the ground, and they occupied a small printer at the rear of the Nook, to keep the newspaper in circulation.

The Fevrier house is a hidden gem—literally—tucked away from the road. In addition to having a spectacular exterior, the interior is even more breathtaking. Inside the home are impressive finishes, doors, windows and shutters. Sadly today, this type of detail cannot be duplicated.

Mr. Fevrier and his mother love this house, it reminds him of his childhood. He wishes to maintain the character and integrity of the house and preserve it in any way possible.

Left: When I asked for permission to take pictures of interior details, Mr. Fevrier and his mother asked if they could be taken as well, "We are the interior details my dear!" they laughed.

Right: These outward swinging double doors date back to the original construction of the house, almost ninety years old. Undoubtedly, these are handmade. The plastic marley flooring is a recent addition.

grass street

OWNER: ALEXANDER FAMILY | CONSTRUCTED: UNKNOWN

The Alexander family home is one of the most impressive houses in Castries. Sitting on Grass Street, those who know this house have fond memories about its history. The Honourable Sir Darnley Alexander C.F.R C.B.E Lord Chief Justice of Nigeria was born in Saint Lucia and lived in this house. He migrated to England to study law in the forties or early fifties, and later took up a position in Nigeria. Well-known, Alexander rose to the position of Chief Justice, even retaining the position through successive military governments. The dedication to his profession was rewarded when he received knighthood from Queen Elizabeth II.

Sir Darnley passed away in 1988 where a state funeral was held for him in Lagos, Nigeria. To celebrate his achievements the Nigerian law school awards graduates with the Sir Darnley Alexander Prize for outstanding performance. In addition to this, the Sir Darnley Alexander Building on Bay Street, in Soufrière, was built and dedicated to him.

The Alexander home is one and a half stories; the half story appears to be loft space with one or two rooms. Detailed fretwork adorns the eaves, and a circular rose window sits within its gable end. From the exterior, a visible space where a steeple may have existed can be seen. Perhaps it was damaged over time and removed from the roof. Intricate fretwork occurs over windows and doors for ventilation purposes. The house has undergone a few minor changes of doors and windows, but remains generally intact. It is said that there used to be planter boxes around the dwelling's perimeter, housing tall and beautiful grasses. This is how Grass Street got its name.

Many houses have a gap within fretwork or eave where the steeple sat prominently in the past.

ti kay nou: an uplifting journey through our tiny Saint Lucian houses

the anse la raye quarter | quatier de lanslawé

The village of Anse La Raye seems to have been named in early French colonial days. On the 1758 map one finds the bay marked Anse de la Raye. Raye is the French word for a fish called a skate. Lefort de Latour states in his description of this place that the name Raye was given to the quarter, "on count of the quantity of fish of this species found in the bay where the town/village is situated."

Anse la Raye is home to the notorious Fish Fry celebration, which occurs every Friday night in the tiny fishing village. Visitors and locals crowd Anse la Raye for fresh seafood, music and local brews. While the rest of the village sits in the shadows, Front Street transforms into a large street party with local brews, music and entertainment.

The houses within Anse la Raye have evolved from the time of early settlers; however, a feature which remained constant is the steep gabled roof, still evident today. The main streetscape displays simple houses built of wood or concrete, ranging in age; newly constructed concrete dwellings are intertwined with wooden vernacular houses. Houses are in close proximity to each other, with small alleyways between them. These alleys allow for pedestrian traffic and access to the buildings in the rear, to provide access to houses tucked in behind other homes.

Two notable structures in the village are the Nativity of the Blessed Virgin Mary Roman Catholic Church and the other the Adjodah House. Built in 1890, the two story rectangular Adjodah House was constructed without the use of nails, but instead builders used wooden pegs. The structure features jalousie windows equipped with well-designed shutters, both of which are constructed of timber. It has a multiple gable roof with fretted fascia's and steeples, wooden columns, handcrafted fretwork and a wooden pad foundation. The Nativity of the Blessed Virgin Mary Roman Catholic Church was built in 1907, but records show that a chapel has existed since 1765. The outside of the church boundary wall has a 150 foot long mural depicting scenes of village life which was donated and painted by the St. Omer family.

Since the village of Anse la Raye is particularly vulnerable to flooding, the Government of Saint Lucia has passed a new building code which forces new constructed houses to be raised three feet off the ground. Anse la Raye's main thoroughfare, Mole Street, demonstrates the variation in architectural styles along its quarter-mile length. The northern end bustles with activity—rum shops, grocery stores and street vendors. The last few blocks are more residential and picturesque, featuring a continuous row of traditional vernacular houses that are over 100 years old.

30 church street

OWNER: JONAH GEORGE | CONSTRUCTED: 1928

"The water was *this* high during Debby," he said, as he pointed to his shoulder. He was standing tall in the doorway, already 2 feet off the ground. "My neighbor was holding on to the shutter there to try to save herself." I closed my eyes and tried to imagine what a natural disaster like that would be like. Tropical Storm Debby struck Saint Lucia in 1994, and wind gusts on the island reached 46 mph. Debby produced heavy rainfall and thunderstorms over a six-hour period, which caused flooding along rivers and in low-lying areas. High rainfall combined with deforestation on hillsides, caused massive landslides and forced over 100 people to evacuate to shelters. Roadways were washed out, and many bridges were severely damaged. Heavy rains covered Hewanorra International Airport with 2 inches of silt, and in Anse La Raye, floods reached waist-deep levels. In that town, residents had to be rescued by boat. Then how can this be, that this tiny house stood tall, while houses around it got carried away by the flood waters?

Jonah George, 35, now resides in this house with his girlfriend and two children. His father built this house when he was a young man, to house his young family. Jonah's best guess is the house is over 85 years old, constructed around 1928.

"I'll tell you why this house is still standing, look at these pegs..." he points up to the rafters, and there are wooden pegs joining beams together—instead of nails. Peg construction allows buildings to warp and bend without falling apart. Their modern cousins, the steel nail, would wiggle out of place, break or rust in the event of an earthquake or hurricane. His wife points to two posts, one original, and one replaced less than 10 years ago. "Guess which one is the old one," she says giggling. One tattered, covered with termites and barely standing; the other, solid, strong and no sign of wear at all. To pull her leg, I decide to go with the old ratty looking post. She shrieked, "I knew you were going to pick that one! You're wrong! This is the old board!" as she pointed to the pristine wooden post.

Although the house shows obvious signs of wear and tear; its boards infested with termites, and the original galvanize finally corroding, Jonah keeps the house the way it is, because he has no choice. He is unemployed, and repairs older model TVs and radios. He fixes the house one piece at a time, when he has the time and resources.

As I said goodbye, Jonah's wife and children waved me goodbye. I was reminded of the simplicity of life, and the shelter this house has provided throughout the years to this family. The Ti Kay even in its dilapidated state, is a basic shelter for many.

the canaries quarter | quatier de kannawi

The 1758 map marks les Canaris between Anse de la Verdure and Ance Mahaut. Lefort de Latour's map shows Anse de Canaries and Riviere des Canaries at the appropriate places. The Admiralty map of 1888 has Anse des Canaries for the bay, Canaries (or two friends) for the village and Piton Canaries. What then is this unusual name? Latour's description does not solve the problem. It has been suggested that the name may have Amerindian origin. The Arawak and/or Caribs used to call one of their cooking vessels by a similar name – Kanaree.

Canaries is a small fishing village nestled along the West Coast road, between Anse La Raye and Soufrière. To the north and south are high headlands—a sheer drop, that extends out into a body of water—that enclose the village. To the west is the Caribbean Sea, and there are scenic views from both the Northern and Southern approaches. Records show that Canaries has existed since 1758 and the original settlers came from the neighboring island of Martinique.

In 1876 a Catholic School was established in the village. After 1929, an infant and junior school were established. When the price of sugar dropped in the middle of the 20th Century, many sugar estates closed in the area, and residents left Canaries to look for work, some reaching as far as the Americas and the United Kingdom. This mass emigration created an increase in capital for Canaries residents, for many of the dispersed sent money back to their families. Intern, they built new houses and established local businesses in the village. Many who owned or inherited vernacular houses lost interest in their old colonial style, and grew fond of modern concrete construction—causing many examples of vernacular architecture to be destroyed or abandoned.

A walk through Canaries reveals tiny houses built close to the street's edge, with some front doors that open within inches of the main road. Dwellings are built close together, and there are small shops and stores woven into the neighborhood. In the heat of the day, there are not very many places to seek shelter from the sweltering sun; however, some residents "lime" in Canaries' main square or in a waterside bar waiting on the local catch of the day. Canaries' St. Anthony Roman Catholic Church dominates the landscape of the town. The interior village of Canaries is not a popular stopping point for locals or visitors; most drive through without ever setting foot into the main village.

Plans for tourism development in the village of Canaries have been underway for many years. Proposals include the refurbishment of the village square and a focus on art, beginning with the renovation of a 100-year-old church into an art gallery.

a riveting journey through our tiny Saint Lucian houses

the soufrière quarter | quatier de soufwiyè

For the early French colonists, the volcanoes, regardless of dormancy, of the Antilles were called Soufrières—places from which sulphur could be extracted. The volcanoes of Guadeloupe, St.. Kitts, and St.. Vincent were also given this name. A 1771 plan of Soufrière labels it "suplphureus mountain: as the volcano—le volcan." The plan actually has an illustration which seems to indicate an eruption.

Soufrière has long been referred to as the breadbasket of Saint Lucia and it is easy to see why—verdant and fertile it was historically home to some of the most productive colonial plantations, and today produces crops of cocoa, citrus, and vegetables. Soufrière abounds in historic architecture and landmarks also, including the Morne Coubaril and Fond Doux Estates. The world famous Pitons, Saint Lucia's most iconic natural attraction, occurs here. The two remarkable volcanic formations jutting dramatically from the sea to form a mountainous skyline became a United Nations Education, Scientific, and Cultural Organization (UNESCO) World Heritage Site in 2004. The Sulphur Springs, known as the world's only "drive-in volcano," are one of Soufrière's most popular attractions. It is from these springs that Soufrière takes its name. In 1784, the dark and pungent waters were tested, and found to possess similar medicinal properties to the waters of the Aix les Bains in France, prompting then Governor Baron de Laborie to build the Diamond Baths. Today, only traces of the original baths can be found at Sulphur Springs.

Over the years, Soufrière has had to deal with hurricanes in 1780, 1817, 1831, 1898 and 1980, a major fire in 1955 and an earthquake in 1991. Many of these events have had to result in the town being rebuilt several times. Even with this, the town has managed to retain its colonial charm and evidence of the influence in the architecture of its old houses and businesses. The Quarter of Soufrière has the largest stock of vernacular architecture on the island. The Roman Catholic Church remains the dominant and focal point of the town which extends to the waterfront, an active harbor for fishermen and boaters.

Home to some of the most luxurious and exclusive hotels on the island, Soufrière has become a destination for tourists and visitors. Due to the influx of interest, the Soufrière Development Foundation was formed with the goal of promoting coordinated development for the Soufrière quarter by creating socially acceptable, sustainable and economically beneficial tourism-related programs and amenities. To date, the foundation is best known for its development of the Sulphur Springs Park, construction of the Soufrière jetties and waterfront, and an extensive inventory of the quarter's heritage resources.

5 high street

OWNER: JOHN SIMON AKA JAH LAMB
CONSTRUCTED: UNKNOWN

If you're a Rastafarian or vegan in Saint Lucia, you must know about Jah Lamb located in Soufrière. An institution for whole living and Ital food, Jah Lamb is small casual eatery that caters to the Rastafarian community as well as vegetarians and vegans.

Jah Lamb's restaurant is a small, green, wooden house in the heart of old Soufrière. The house, passed on to him from his grandmother is in unrenovated condition, and has become an essential stop for locals and tourists. His kitchen is decorated with articles about vegetarianism and posters and newspaper cuttings about famous Rastafarians—Bob Marley, Haile Selassie and Buju Banton. It's a quaint eatery, with tables covered in plastic mats, photos all over the walls and a TV in the middle of the room; a modern addition he doesn't mind. The kitchen is open to view Jah Lamb cooking delicious treats.

Soft spoken and extremely humble, Ras Jah Lamb was magnetic, and had wisdom beyond his years. Somehow, I knew his given name of Ras Jah Lamb had something to do with his demeanor. I had to ask how he got it.

ti kay nou: an uplifting journey through our tiny Saint Lucian houses

"My friends gave me the name Jah Lamb; they say I am calm, understanding, patient and humble. When I was seven years old and my grandmother started to teach me how to look after myself. You can be independent and look after yourself and teach the other people who come after you, but you must do it patiently, with humility."

Before we started talking about the house, we talked about the food; Ital. "I use a very traditional style of cooking. There is only coconut cream in my food, my grandmother showed me how to make it—the old people used to call it *mapa*. My ingredients come from organic farmers around here. All my seasoning is local, ti lonyon (scallion), seasoning peppers, lots of garlic, sweet peppers, piment manjak (scotch bonnet peppers)... everything local and all vegetarian. This lifestyle makes you live longer and healthier." Nearby, a sign read "meat's no treat for those you eat," making me really regret all the meat patties I had hours before...

Jah Lamb's grandmother was willed this house by an elderly man she used to take care of when he passed away. His grandmother raised him here, and when she passed, she willed the house to him. The house is in its original state, except for a few new boards placed at the northern façade due to water runoff; he's wanted to keep the house as authentic as possible. "I love it here, I wake up at 5 every morning to start preparing for the day," he must have seen the quizzical look on my face, because I couldn't understand that he lived in the restaurant too! But where? He closes the restaurant, and directs me to follow him through the kitchen and up a winding staircase to his home upstairs. A small and quaint loft space, plastered with posters, ites, green and gold emblems and flags, and dormer windows open above the street to the sky. I immediately wanted to move in. He pointed to the wooden pegs, which held the rafters together securely for over 80 years.

Unfortunately, the house is in need of roofing repairs, and newer more modern galvanize is being installed. It is Jah Lamb's hope that the pegs and rafters can be saved amidst the renovation. We finished up the tour in his backyard, where he pointed to uncovered earth where he wanted to plant a small garden. When he first started, he noticed coal pieces and ashes, indicating that either the previous owner made or sold coals in the back yard.

Considering that the house has been exposed to the harsh conditions of the tropics throughout its existence, it seems to be in fairly reasonable condition. The elements of rain and wind have battered the wooden boards, and the repeated wetting and drying of the timber over decades have caused them to decay, split and warp.

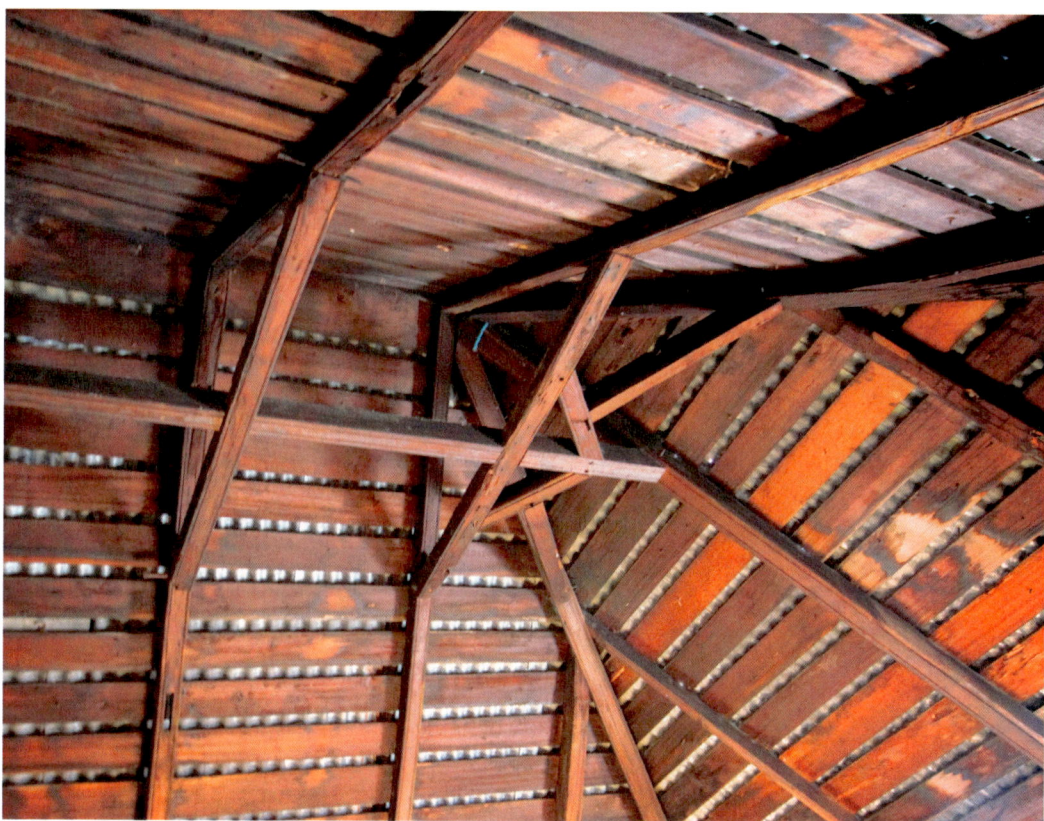

Top: Original wooden pegs hold wooden rafters in place for over eighty years. Jah Lamb isn't sure of the type of wood used. **Left:** The preparation area for Jah Lamb's cooking begins outside. He kneads dough, minces seasonings and grates coconuts for **mapa**. **Far Left:** The entire space is decorated in ites, green and gold imagery and trinkets. Ites refers to the colour red which is the uppermost colour of the Rastafarian Ethiopian flag or red (ites), gold and green flown by the Nyabinghi theocracy.

ti **kay nou**: an uplifting journey through our tiny Saint Lucian houses

boulevard street

OWNER: MARIE GUSTAVE AKA MS. COOK | CONSTRUCTED: 1933

After taking a few pictures and explaining what we were doing to a young man, he said, "If you're looking for an old house, go inside there..." I have been to Soufrière hundreds of times, and each time I find or learn something new. This day I would find a peculiar house, in a strange location, down an alley and past stranger's houses...

Her name is Marie Gustave, and her house, standing in an alley, and tucked behind a peculiar row of houses, was built by her father in 1933. "They call me Ms. Cook because I used to cook for the priests in the presbytery, for forty years" She retired at the age of 61.

A jovial woman, Ms. Cook, as she would like to be called, is bed ridden now, but filled with fond memories of the house. "I carried wood on my head! All the way from Fond St.. Jacques to build this house." I tried to map the distance in my mind from Fond St.. Jacques to Boulevard Street—and realized it had to be at least three to four miles away. She was seventeen years old at the time.

The house was built in pieces in Font St.. Jacques, by three men; Clement Gustave, Raymond Clovis and Zavier. Her memory is still sharp.

It was assembled on site, and put together with wooden pegs – still visible and in-tact today. All four corners of the house are braced with cross-braces, making it sturdy for years to come.

It has survived through notable hurricanes, namely hurricane Allen, when mostly everything was flattened around it. The galvanize has been the only thing changed on Cook's house, "since this house was built, the galvanize hasn't been changed. Recently, I had to change a piece it. Now, the new galvanize looks older than the original galvanize, which has been around for over eighty years."

Left: The entrance to Ms. Cook's house remains the same, as the day it was built. She remembers carpenters bringing pictures from an old French book to show her father; they claimed they could replicate them. A few weeks later, the doors arrived, and they are standing and operable, eighty years later.

ti kay nou: an uplifting journey through our tiny Saint Lucian houses | 85

ti kay nou: an uplifting journey through our tiny Saint Lucian houses | 87

the chosieul quarter | quatier de chawzèy

Choiseul was originally known as Anse Citron, and an independent parish was established in 1765. The village was named Anse Choiseul in honour of the Duke of Choiseul, French Minister for Foreign Affairs. This was later shortened to 'Choiseul'.

Choiseul, one of the largest quarters on the island, is well known for its arts and crafts. These traditional practices have been passed down for centuries, with historians tracing their origins to the original settlers, the Carib and Arawak Indians. The Choiseul Arts and Craft Centre is a local centre where visitors and locals learn more about these crafts, support local artisans or to pick up unique souvenirs. The centre is largely used by artisans in the community, who come together to sell their products; woven baskets, chairs, grass mats, coconut and wood carvings, pottery and children's toys.

Choiseul showcases ancient petroglyphs carved centuries ago by the islands Amerindian inhabitants. One of the most popular sites in Choiseul is the Balenbouche Estate. Balenbouche is a 75 acre estate featuring a 200-year-old wooden plantation house in its original state. The name Balenbouche is translated from French to mean 'bullet in the mouth' alluding to a legend of a duel fought here between two sailors over the hand of a woman. Created as a cotton plantation in the early 1700s the estate switched to sugar in 1780 when machinery was imported from England to create a water-powered sugar factory that is now in ruins. The Balenbouche Estate contains both Amerindian ceramics and several significant petroglyphs, all of which have undergone thorough examination by the Saint Lucia Archeological and Historic Society. These works of art by Saint Lucia's early Amerindian ancestors have been deemed among the most archeologically important on the island. The estate was transformed into a Heritage Tourism Site, eco-lodge, and organic farm. The plantation house is nearly 200 years old and holds great history and antiques.

One of the most famous stories in Saint Lucia's folklore—"The Devil's Bridge"—occurred in Choiseul. To understand this story, you have to understand the location of the bridge: It spans a 60-meter deep ravine in the River Dorée area. Legend has it that the man who built it made a pact with the devil. He promised that when the bridge was finished, the devil could take the first soul who walked over it. When the bridge was completed, the man sent his little dog ahead, to cheat the devil. They say the dog disappeared into thin air and was never seen again. Ever since then it has been called the Devil's Bridge.

Surounding notable structures include the Anglican Church which dates back to 1846. Its French inspired presbytery has a steep, pyramidal corrugated-iron roof, attic dormer windows and heavy storm shutters. Chosieul's main village is tiny in comparison to others around the island, because of this, most of the vernacular structures which exist along the main street—High Street—are concentrated. A delightful mix of establishements and building types occur along High Street.

ti kay nou: an uplifting journey through our tiny Saint Lucian houses

high street

S. MICHAEL'S BAR | OWNER: UNKNOWN
CONSTRUCTED: UNKNOWN

It's hard not to notice these two tiny houses along High Street in Chosieul. The S. Michael Bar, with its green detailed overhang, has a cross-brace near the top of the gable end. The style could have been adopted and changed to mimic the steeple, found commonly in that era. There is a louvered window in the gable roof, with fixed slats for constant ventilation. The door is slightly off centre, and there is a tiny window. I could just imagine the interesting nights (and quite possibly days) in this tiny rum bar.

The building to the right appears to be less suited for commercial use; perhaps a small home for someone who lived in the country side. It shares similar features to its neighbor – narrow front, cross-brace near the top of the gable roof. The door is on centre, with two windows flanking each side. There is a small overhang across the entire length of the tiny house, I assume for shade and to escape the rain. As most Saint Lucians love island politics, this house wouldn't be complete without political party posters plastered on its front!

ti kay nou: an uplifting journey through our tiny Saint Lucian houses

the laborie quarter | quatier de labowi

Formerly known as Rade et Anse de l'Ilet a Caret, meaning Turtle Island Anchorage and Beach, the village was renamed in honour of the Baron de Laborie, Governor of Saint Lucia from 1784 to 1789.

Laborie became an independent parish in 1765. By 1775, houses had appeared, along with the first church, and 81 estates throughout the quarter had been given to French settlers. Some of these settlers' names live on in the names of the small communities, such as Augier and Banse. By 1780, Laborie was one of the main settlements in Saint Lucia, supporting the second largest population after Soufrière.

Most residents lived inland, or 'in the country' where they farmed. On weekends, they came down into Laborie Village to sell produce and attend church services. Roads were difficult to traverse then; travel to other communities or to the capital of Castries took place by boat and ferry.
In 1838 the Mico School was opened. It was the first school in Laborie, and was opened and operated by the Lady Mico Trust; it had 80 pupils and closed its doors in 1891. By this time a new Catholic school had opened in the village.

As recently as then end of WWII, Laborie did not have electricity, or pipe-borne water. In the 1950's, Morne Le Blanc in Laborie was the site of an American radar station, which necessitated creating better infrastructure, including a new road from Vieux Fort to Laborie and up the Morne. The station also protected the Beane Army Airfield which is now the Hewanorra International Airport. Remnants of the airfield are still visible today.

Most if not all of the structures in the Laborie community are constructed of timber and feature gable roofs. These houses are rectangular in shape, with wooden columns, and some have a shingled exterior. Throughout the village, there are a number of houses that have been in existence from 49 to 120 years. Because of this, there are varying states of disrepair.

la croix road

OWNER: THE LOUISY FAMILY | CONSTRUCTED: 1930
CONTRIBUTED BY HER EXCELLENCY DAME PEARLETTE LOUISY

The family house stands on a parcel of land measuring 31 feet wide by 82 feet deep, dismembered from what was known as the Mon Repos Estate in the parish of Laborie in 1895 for the then princely sum of three pounds twelve shillings sterling. However, there seems to be no record of when the structure was built, except that it became the main family home from 1930. It is a two-bedroom house, with a living room, a pantry and an attic which served as the main sleeping area for most of the family. The roof and sidings were originally covered with wood shingles, but in the 1950's galvanized roofing was installed and asphalt shingles replaced the original ones on the western, southern and eastern facades. The original shingles on the northern façade still remain.

The house has weathered many a hurricane: Hurricane Janet in the 1950's, Hurricane Allen in 1980 and Hurricane Tomas in 2010 were perhaps the strongest and most memorable. It still remains amazingly solid due in large measure perhaps to the use of pegs and dowels , rather than nails, its siting and its general architecture.. During Hurricane Tomas it took just the combined efforts of two female members of the family to keep it steady as it rocked and creaked under the pressure of Category 1 – force winds.!

It has served as home to four generations, with very little repair done to it, except for the replacement of the original wooden exterior flight of steps by a concrete structure. Family members fondly refer to it as "the Museum", but are still unclear as to what should be done to or with it.

ti kay nou: an uplifting journey through our tiny Saint Lucian houses

ti kay nou: an uplifting journey through our tiny Saint Lucian houses | 103

ti kay nou: an uplifting journey through our tiny Saint Lucian houses | 107

the vieux fort quarter | quatier de vyé fò

Inhabitants built forts to protect themselves from unwanted raids. One of these forts was located at Point Sables, in the town of Vieux Fort. After sometime, it was abandoned, but the ruins remained. That was how Vieux Fort got its name, for in English Vieux Fort means 'old fort'.

Dotted with several small communities surrounding Saint Lucia's second-largest town, the region of Vieux Fort is amply gifted with a combination of historic sites and cultural offerings. The former centre of Saint Lucia's sugar industry, the town of Vieux Fort is a curious juxtaposition of the industrially modern with the distinctly colonial. Saint Lucia's main point of entry for visitors, the Hewanorra Airport is located here.

During the Second World War, Vieux Fort became a base for American troops. Some of the evidence can still be seen around town, such as the underground tunnel that runs from Clark Street to the old St. Jude Hospital. This tunnel was used for storage of supplies and also a quick route to the hospital. Many people who reside in Vieux Fort today have no idea that this tunnel exists!

In recent years a new modern part of Vieux Fort has been erected to reflect the modern world, yet Clark Street and surrounding roads bear resemblance to the old town. Here, a few examples of traditional vernacular houses have survived, but are in various states of disrepair.

A notable tourist attraction is the Maria Islands Nature Reserve, managed by the Saint Lucia National Trust, which is a nesting ground for leatherback turtles and is home to a species of iguana indigenous to St. Lucia. The world's second highest lighthouse, Moule a Chic lighthouse is also located near here, standing on a 730-foot hill.

24 lewis street

OWNER: MARGUARITE ALEXANDER
CONSTRUCTED: 1943

Tucked away in the old town of Vieux Fort lies the most beautiful and well-preserved example of traditional vernacular architecture. I had visited the house while the owner was away, and a neighbor happily gave me a telephone number for Ms. Margaurite Alexander, after I explained the Ti Kay Nou project.

    Ms. Alexander has maintained this house since her parent's passing a few years ago. Her father, the original builder, had no experience as an architect. He relied on pattern books and pictures of French houses from neighboring Martinique, and built the house for both function and form.

ti kay nou: an uplifting journey through our tiny Saint Lucian houses

"I love this house, people say it's old, but I am in love with it," she says to me over the telephone. Margaurite was excited about the idea of reviving historic preservation on the island; many have approached and complimented her on this house, but she never thought anybody cared about it enough. "Anybody can build a house these days, they don't even need to know how to draw, far less have any skills." We had a lengthy discussion about the way houses were being built of concrete and block—and as we both agree that St. Lucia shouldn't revert to its colonial days, we should seek to 'borrow' ideas and elements of the past, which have been adapted to our way of life and climate.

Ms. Alexander's house is one and a half stories, and is elevated three feet from the ground to spare its inhabitants from flood waters. It also adds privacy; pedestrians can't see directly into the dwelling from the road. The verandah is as wide as the house, and is ten feet deep—making it large enough to host friends and family for any occasion. Painted in a charming yellow with burgundy accents, the house has contrastingly stark white fretwork along the balustrades.

The ground floor of the Alexander house hosts all family rooms; kitchen, formal living room and drawing room. Stairs lead to the upper portion of the house where the bedrooms are located. The house also boasts four steeples. When I told Ms. Alexander the story behind the steeples, their function, and the number of steeples occurring around the dwelling, she replied, "That would explain why nothing bad has ever happened in this house!" I guess we will never know…

Ms. Alexander is one of many who wish to preserve and maintain our architectural heritage through programs which incentivise initiatives to do so.

Top: Intricate fretwork adorns the dwelling's exterior. Marguarite mentioned that she can't find very many carpenters in Saint Lucia with the skill of duplicating or creating fretwork. She has often had to get the designs custom made in neighboring Dominica.

ti kay nou: an uplifting journey through our tiny Saint Lucian houses | 113

the micoud quarter | quatier de mikou

Micoud was named after Baron de Micoud, who was the French governor of Saint Lucia in the 18th Century.

Of all quarters on the island, Micoud is the richest in Amerindian history. It is home to almost 3,000 residents, who have proudly preserved the local traditions. Between Micoud and Canelles, archaeologists have found evidence of eight or nine settlements. Remains of cooking pits, tools, pots, and ornaments have been discovered at Troumasse, Micoud Bay, and Anse Capitaine. Artifacts have also been found on the banks of the River Ger and on the two headlands of the Canelles River. Why is the Amerindian history so rich in this part of the island? Many texts point to the topography of the village, its sloping coastline, sheltered bays and flowing rivers—including the Troumassée River—which made it attractive to settlers. Much of the land north of Micoud ends in high jagged cliffs.

In recent history, Micoud was the constituency of Sir John Compton, who was the Premier of Saint Lucia from 1967-1979, then Prime Minister in 1979, 1982-1996 and 2006-2007.

Micoud boasts natural attractions like the 20-foot high Latille waterfall, with its natural freshwater pools that surround it; and the nearby Mamiku Gardens, with an explosion of colour thanks to its hundreds of flowers, orchids, and butterfly species.

Like many other towns and villages in Saint Lucia, Micoud's vernacular houses are in a state of disrepair and decay. Many of the structures are abandoned, which leads the thought that they have been passed down to younger generations who aren't aware of their potential value.

the dennery quarter | quatier de dennwi

Lefort de Latour has Pointe et anse d'Ennery on his map. The spelling d'Ennery was retained on the Admiralty map of 1888. The fact is, the quarter, bay, headland and village take their name from Count d'Ennery, who was Governor General of the French Windward Islands in 1786, when St.. Lucia was re-annexed to Martinique. The district, says LDL, was formerly called l'Anse Canot et le grand Mabouya. Incidentally, he presented a chalice and paten to the parish of St.. Lucia that took his name.

Before Dennery took the count's name, it had been called Anse Canot. Canoes, carved from the Gommier trees' large trunks, were brought down the river to the coast of Dennery to be launched. A neighborhood in the village is still called Anse Canot. A wide valley nearby, which stretches into to the forest, is known as the Grand Mabouya Valley. It is the largest valley on the east coast of Saint Lucia and the central producer of much of its sugar, rum, and bananas. A labyrinth of secret trails, tracks, and concealed paths, the Mabouya Valley was often trekked by former slaves on their journey to freedom. The Valley is made up of Derniere Riviere, Au Leon, Despinoze, Gadette, Grand Riviere, Grand Ravine, La Ressource, Richfond and other surrounding areas.

In the early days, the Dennery village was a busy place with markets where meat, fish and vegetables were sold. Villagers recall their festive Christmases; streets lit by Coleman Lamps and almost every house had a candle-lit lantern sitting in the window sill. Most of these traditions are gone today; the village has expanded to over 10,000 residents, living in various parts of the Dennery district.

The sleepy fishing village comes to life on Saturday afternoons for its weekly Dennery Fish Fiesta. The beach party starts on Saturday afternoons and doesn't end until the early hours of the morning. A dozen tents line the beach as local DJs play the latest local music. It's a great place for both tourists and locals to sample various local cuisine based primarily on local seafood.

Frigate Island Nature Reserve is offshore a few kilometers to the south of the town. The Saint Lucia National Trust does not allow anyone on the islands, but an easily accessible 1.5 km trail engineered across cliffs and up to an overlook opposite the Islands has a magnificent view. Another popular natural attraction is the Sault Falls, also known as Errard Falls. The falls are over 60-feet tall, where water plummets over a rounded cliff.

Of all the quarters on the island, Dennery shows the most visible signs of vernacular architecture depletion. A walk through the town's streets will reveal modern concrete structures where wooden vernacular architecture once stood. The village has suffered damage from several hurricanes and tropical storms, so they could have been destroyed and replaced with modern homes built to withstand flooding. A few notable houses remain, including the ones shown within the following pages.

glossary

Ajoupa. Amerindian house built on stilts.

Arcade. A series of arches, often in front of a covered passageway.

Balustrade. A low railing either along a balcony or up a stairway.

Bohio. Amerindian word meaning thatched rural house.

Bracket. Projecting wooden structure, supporting eaves.

Case. Basic, wood-built hut or house in the French Islands of the Caribbean.

Casement. Chamber inside the thickness of walls, usually with embrasures.

Chamfer. Bevelled edge, formed by cutting off the square angle.

Chattel House. Name of a small, usually moveable wooden house typically found in Barbados.

Cistern. A depression or structure designed to catch or hold water.

Clapboard. Similar to weather board, employing wooden exterior wall cladding.

Colonnade. Series of columns, usually supporting a roof, verandah or upper storey.

Column. Long, vertical cylinder supporting an arch or entablature.

Cranked. Angled roof line over a verandah.

Cresting. Decoration on a roof ridge.

Crown. Top part of arch or vault.

Demerara windows. Long louvers which hinge outwards from small balcony-like protrusions, like window boxes, often made of wooden latticework. These window projections usually incorporate top-hung shutters which can be opened by means of a wooden strut.

Dormer window. Window built proud the line of the roof.

Dry stone. Construction technique without the use of mortar and cement.

Eave. The underside of a roof overhang.

Entablature. Part of an order above the column, including frieze and cornice.

Façade. Face of the building.

Fanlight. An opening over a doorway in the shape of an open fan.

Fenestration. The arrangement of windows in a building.

Finial. Ornament finishing off the apex of a roof.

Fish-scale tiles. Overlapping tiles common in French tropical buildings.

Flush. On the same plane level as surrounding surfaces.

Gable. Triangular upper part of the wall, at the end of ridged roof.

Gable window. Window located above the roof line of a pitched roof, but with its own small roof.

Gazebo. Small outside shelter, often open-sided and decorative.

Georgian. Classical Palladian symmetrical style, often called Caribbean Georgian.

Gingerbread. Fretwork typical of the Victorian Era, embellishing the outside of a house.

Half-hipped roof. Roof with steeper slopes at the sides than at the ends, which form gables.

Hipped roof. Roof where sides and ends have the same slope from the ridge.

Hurricane shutters. Solid, plain window shutters, barred in place with a thick slotted wooden bar, sometimes ornate on the inside.

Jalousie. Slatted or louvered wooden shutter or blind over a window or door.

Lattice. A crisscross patterning used in screening, or the name for a hinged window, or the pattern on a window creating diamond shapes.

Lintel. Horizontal timber or stone over window or a door.

Louvre. Arrangement of sloping boards designed to shed rain outwards but to let light enter.

Mullion. Vertical bar which separates a window into sections.

Ridge. Line along a roof where the slopes meet.

Shingle. Usually rectangular slats of wood used as roofing or wall tiles.

Vernacular. Architecture indigenous to a country or region.

| protecting saint lucia's built heritage

Saint Lucia Archaeological and Historical Society

Established in 1953, The Archaeological and Historical Society of Saint Lucia has played a defining role in educating Saint Lucians about the importance of archives and museums. Concerned with the island's national and cultural heritage—both above and below ground—the Society purchased and collected historical documents which now form the nucleus of the National Archives Authority of Saint Lucia. In the 1960s the Society set up the first museum which unfortunately no longer exists. The society has continuously been involved in exhibitions, public lectures, publications, and public outreach.

Saint Lucia Archaeological and Historical Society
Coral Street
Castries, Saint Lucia
Tel: 1-758-452-3182

Saint Lucia National Archives Authority of Saint Lucia

The National Archives Authority of Saint Lucia exists to collect, protect preserve and provide access to public and private records, archives and records of national significance, to engage in educational and outreach activities and to promote the use of these records and to advise Government Ministries/ Departments and Statutory Bodies in the area of Records Management.

Saint Lucia National Archives
Clarke Avenue Vigie
Castries, Saint Lucia
Tel: 1-758-452-1654

Saint Lucia National Trust

The Saint Lucia National Trust is a membership organization established in 1979 to conserve the natural and cultural heritage of Saint Lucia, and to promote values which lead to national pride and love of country. The Trust's focus to date has been on the maintenance of these sites as part of the national patrimony, and in advocating the sustainable use and management of Saint Lucia's natural resources. The Trust manages protected areas including National Landmarks, Historical Sites, Environmental Protection Areas and Nature Reserves. The Trust is not only the longest serving environmental and heritage conservation organization on the island, but also the only membership organization with a legal mandate to conserve both the natural and cultural heritage of Saint Lucia.

Saint Lucia National Trust
P.O. Box 595
Castries, Saint Lucia
Tel: 1-758-452-5005

About the Author

Elma Julia Felix is a budding new urbanist, architect and self-taught photographer with a fascination with Saint Lucian history. Born to Saint Lucian parents, she spent most of her childhood in Saint Lucia. A tiny vernacular plantation home in Soufrière, ignited her interest in architecture at an early age. Seeing houses decaying like her beloved family house, transitioned into action, to inspire all to become active in preserving Saint Lucia's built heritage through this publication. Elma has travelled throughout the world, learning from other cultures. She visits Saint Lucia often, making time to photograph and journey off the beaten path. Elma resides in Miami, Florida and can be found rummaging through antique stores and vintage books shops for the things that inspire her.

About the Artist

Shay is a Grenadian-born St. Lucian, who grew up in East Africa. In her early career, she worked with watercolors and textiles and had a successful line of hand-painted children's clothing. However, after suffering a stroke in her early thirties she was forced to redefine her style, and her current medium of choice is acrylics on canvas with a palette knife. Shay's topics are traditional Caribbean scenes are executed with a remarkable vitality in a bright and brazen style, showing an acute understanding of the relationship between color and texture. Her work has been on display in Jamaica, Barbados and St. Lucia and can be seen in numerous private homes around the Caribbean.